SPEAK SOFTLY,
AND CARRY A
BEAGLE

Books by Charles M. Schulz

Peanuts
More Peanuts
Good Grief, More Peanuts!
Good Ol' Charlie Brown
Snoopy
You're Out of Your Mind, Charlie Brown!
But We Love You, Charlie Brown
Peanuts Revisited
Go Fly a Kite, Charlie Brown
Peanuts Every Sunday
It's a Dog's Life, Charlie Brown
You Can't Win, Charlie Brown
Snoopy, Come Home
You Can Do It, Charlie Brown
We're Right Behind You, Charlie Brown
As You Like it, Charlie Brown
Sunday's Fun Day, Charlie Brown
You Need Help, Charlie Brown
Snoopy and the Red Baron
The Unsinkable Charlie Brown
You'll Flip, Charlie Brown
You're Something Else, Charlie Brown
Peanuts Treasury
You're You, Charlie Brown
You've Had It, Charlie Brown
Snoopy and His Sopwith Camel
A Boy Named Charlie Brown
You're Out of Sight, Charlie Brown
Peanuts Classics
You've Come a Long Way, Charlie Brown
· Snoopy and "It Was a Dark and Stormy Night"
"Ha Ha, Herman," Charlie Brown
The "Snoopy, Come Home" Movie Book
Snoopy's Grand Slam
Thompson Is in Trouble, Charlie Brown
You're the Guest of Honor, Charlie Brown
The Snoopy Festival
Win a Few, Lose a Few, Charlie Brown
Speak Softly, and Carry a Beagle

A New **PEANUTS**® Book

SPEAK SOFTLY, AND CARRY A BEAGLE

by Charles M. Schulz

Holt, Rinehart and Winston / New York

Published simultaneously in Canada by Holt, Rinehart
and Winston of Canada, Limited.

First published in book form in 1975.

Library of Congress Catalog Card Number: 75-823

ISBN: 0-03-013851-5

First Edition

Printed in the United States of America

10 9 8 7 6 5 4 3 2

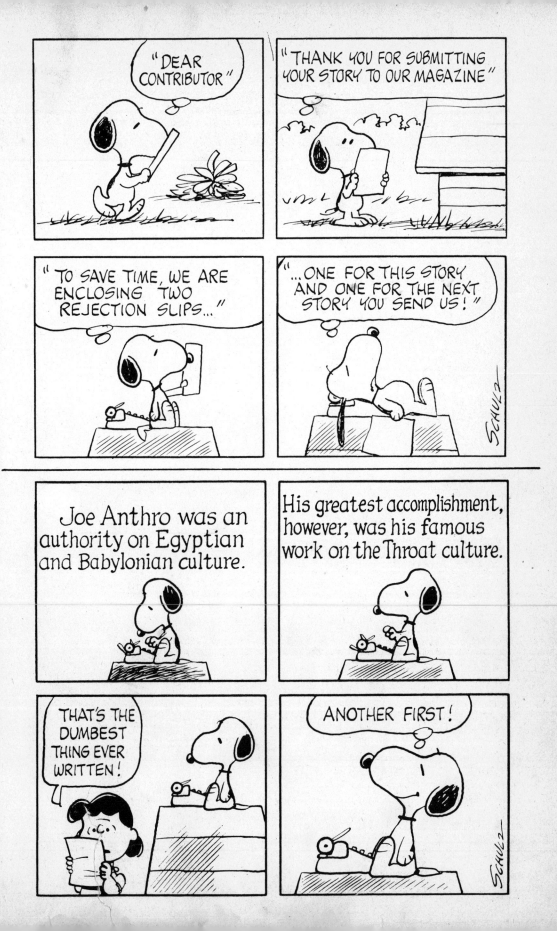

History Report;
Ancient Greece
Ancient Greece wa
ahead of its tim
and before our time
They had no TV,
but they had lots
of philosophers.
I, personally, would
not want to sit all
evening watching
a philosopher.
SCHULZ

MY GRANDFATHER HAS A BIRTHDAY THIS WEEK
DOES HE MIND GETTING OLD?
NO, HE SAYS IT DOESN'T BOTHER HIM... IN FACT, HE SAYS HE FEELS GREAT...
HE SAYS THAT ONCE YOU'RE OVER THE HILL, YOU BEGIN TO PICK UP SPEED!
SCHULZ

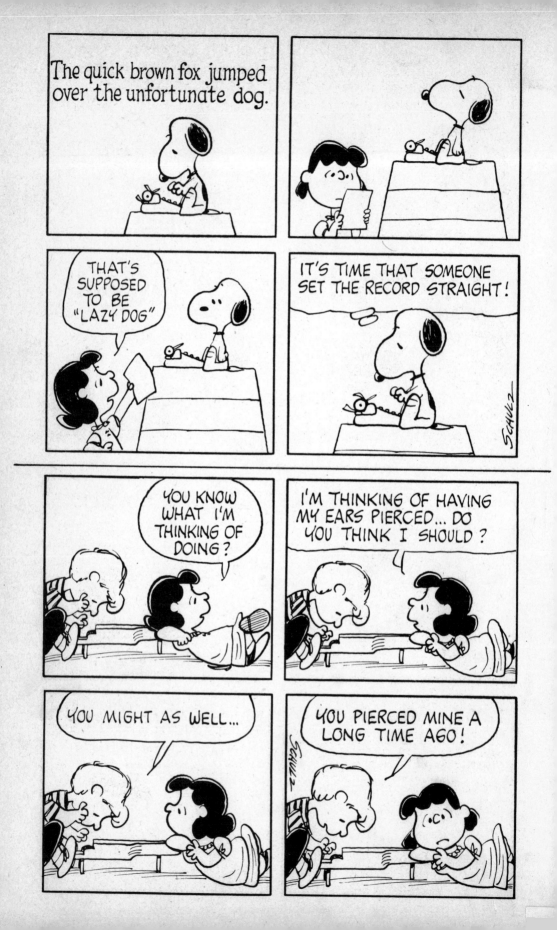

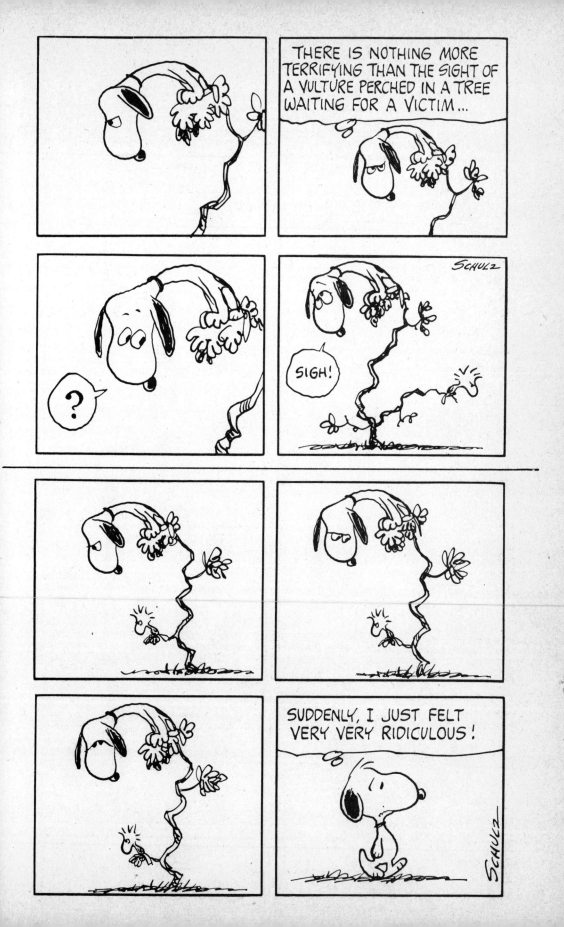

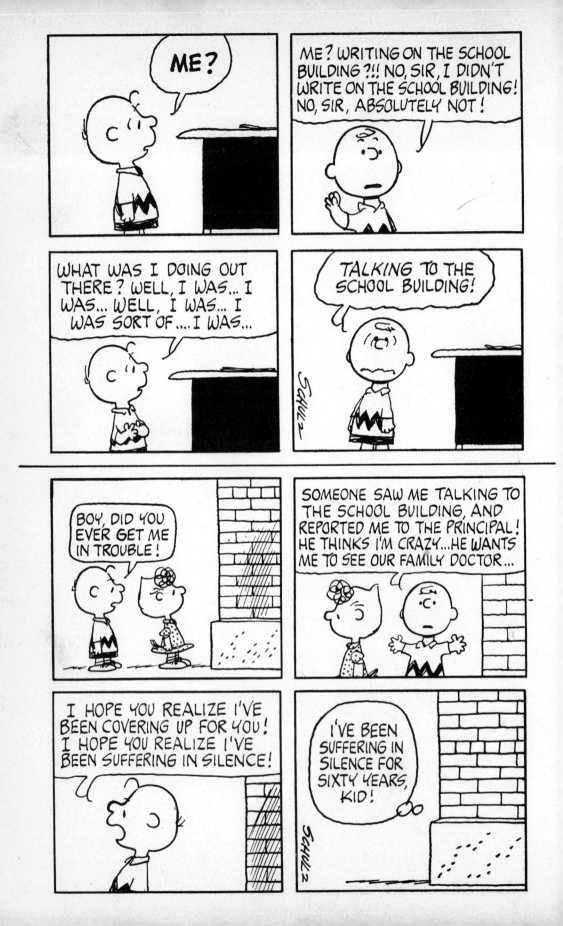

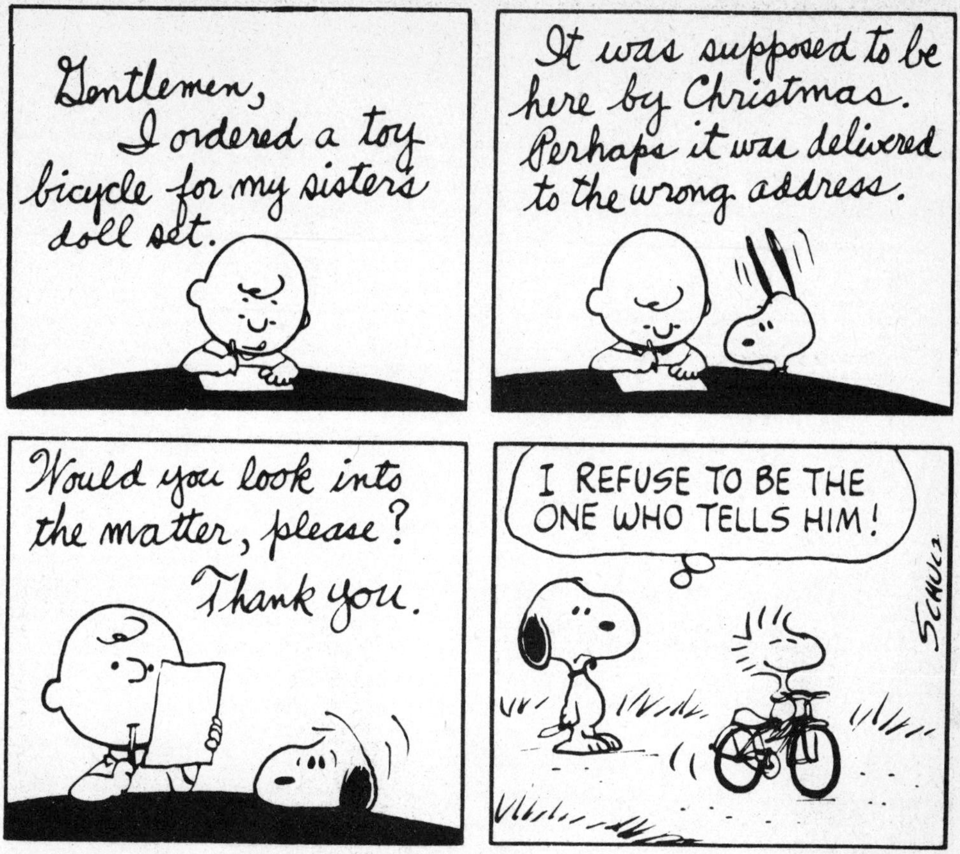
Gentlemen,
I ordered a toy bicycle for my sister's doll set.
It was supposed to be here by Christmas. Perhaps it was delivered to the wrong address.
Would you look into the matter, please?
Thank you.
I REFUSE TO BE THE ONE WHO TELLS HIM!
SCHULZ

I ORDERED A TOY BICYCLE FOR YOUR DOLL SET, BUT IT NEVER CAME...
I HAVE A FEELING IT WAS PROBABLY DELIVERED TO THE WRONG ADDRESS...
WELL, I HOPE WHOEVER GOT IT, ENJOYS IT!!
WHEELIES, YET! GOOD GRIEF!
SCHULZ

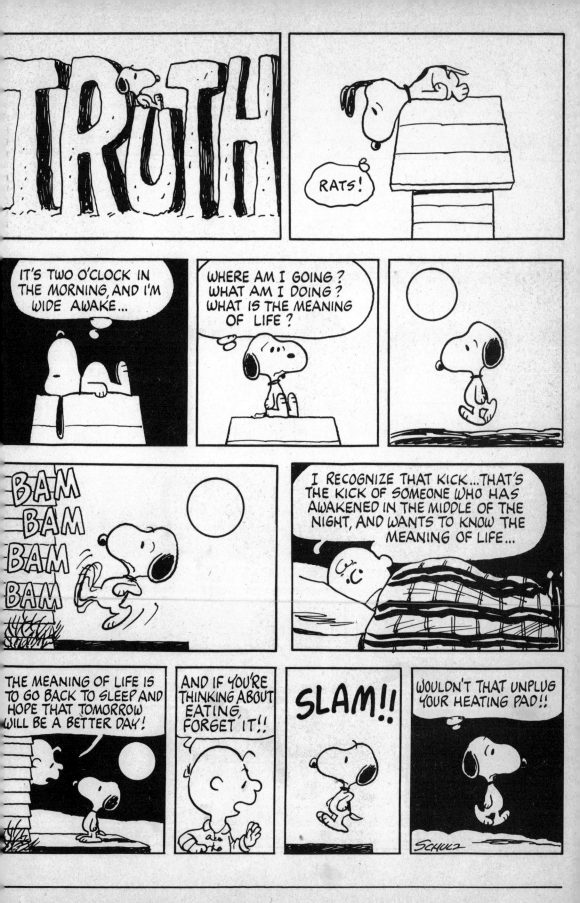

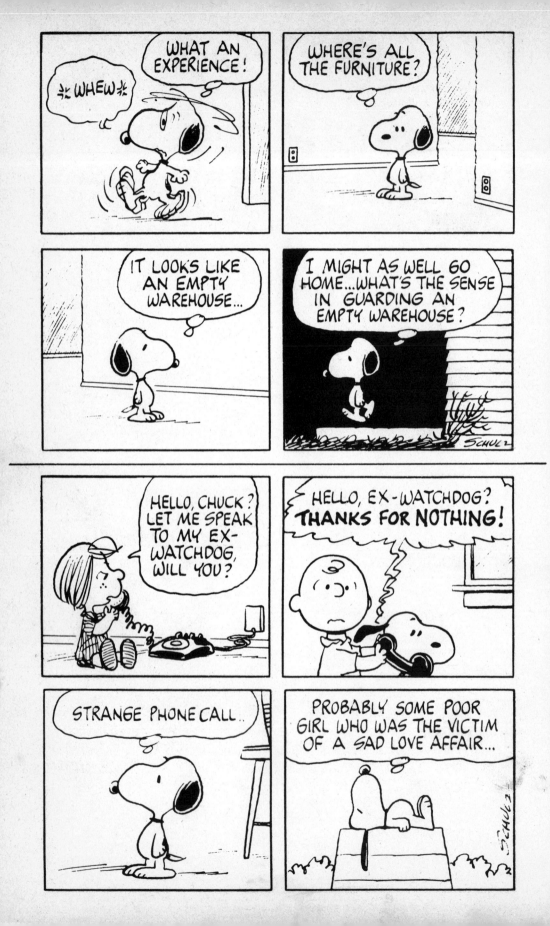